The Thinking Tree

FIRE LIGHT
Art & Logic Therapy
BRAIN GAMES

Mental Clarity, Mindfulness

& Creative Literacy Skills

Book 3

Brain Fog Therapy By Sarah Janisse Brown

Adapted from Dyslexia Games Series B & C to sharpen the minds of individuals suffering from clouded thinking.

The Thinking Tree Publishing Company, LLC

FUNSCHOOLING.COM

Copyright 2022 ~ Reproducible for Family Use Only

PREPARATION:

- Create a calm environment by reducing distractions and setting the mood.
- Enjoy a cup of tea, coffee, water or green lemonade!
- Have coloring supplies and a fine point black pen ready to use.

SCHEDULING OPTIONS:

A. Use 2 pages per day, 6 days a week.
B. Use 3 pages per day, 4 days per week.
C. Use ten pages per week, any number of days.

INSTRUCTIONS:

Look at each page and decide what is missing.
Finish the pattern, solve the puzzle, or use logic to complete the picture.
Add color as you relax and listen to peaceful music. Coloring gives your brain time to process the therapy.

HOW THE GAMES WORK:

The pages include highly detailed drawing activities, number games, word and letter games, and logic puzzles. This book focuses on word games. The words in this book are the top 150 misspelled words in the English language.

The games were originally created to create new connections in the brains of dyslexic students. These same connections can help anyone to create new mental pathways for optimum brain function and healthy synapses. The idea is simple. When you do a new activity your brain is forced to create new pathways. These activities will be unfamiliar to your brain at first. Some pages may seem simple, some may seem confusing and complicated. The idea is to give your brain a workout as you combine creativity, logic, symbols, literacy, and problem solving in a fresh way.

CREATE AN ENVIRONMENT OF NOURISHMENT AND PEACE

Do what it takes to create an environment where you can thrive.

Choose at least two of these prompts each day to help you set the stage for focus and calm. Once you have made a positive change in your surroundings you may begin.

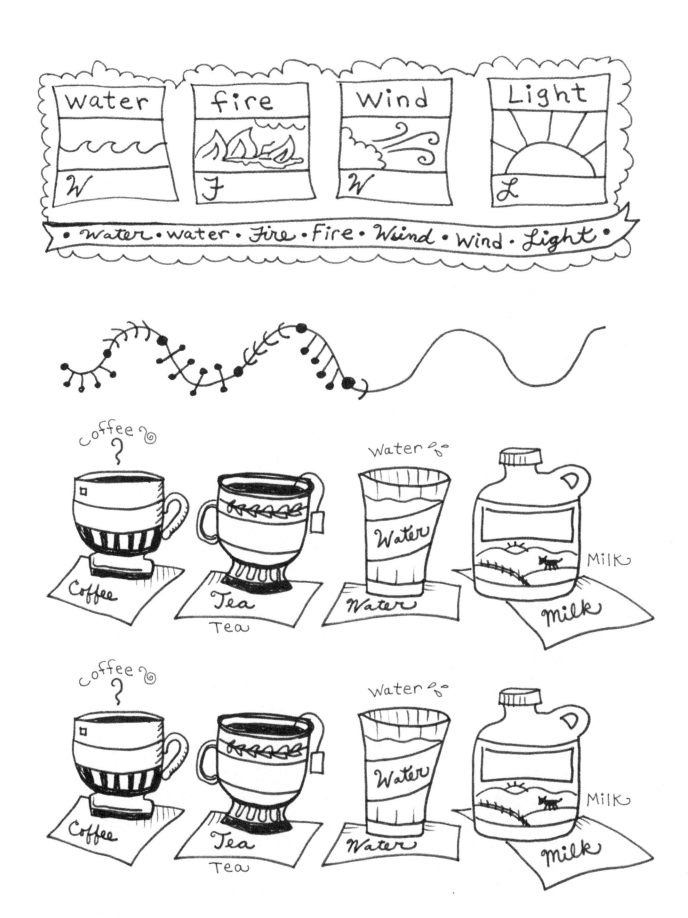

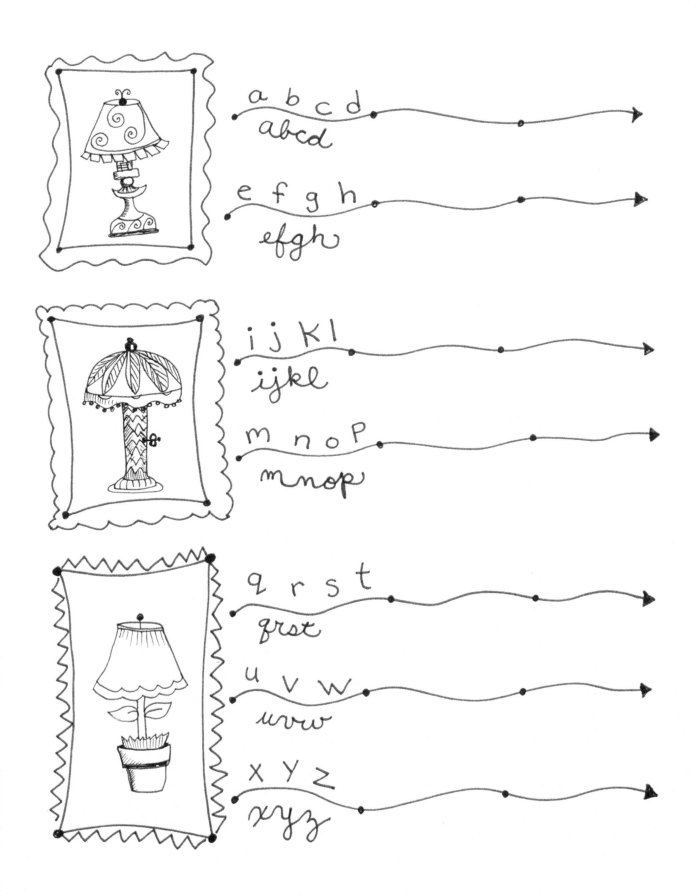

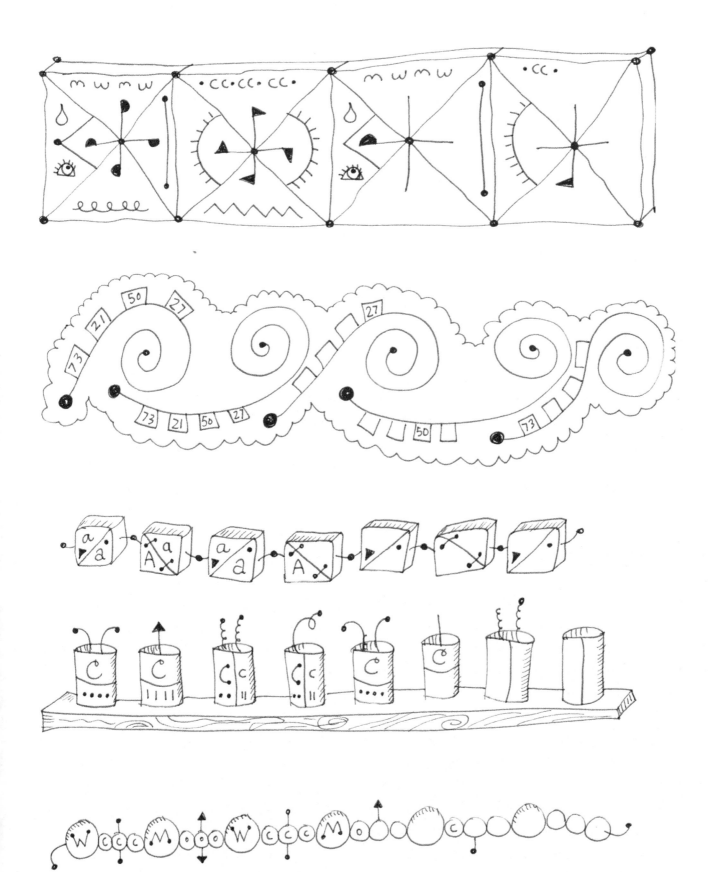

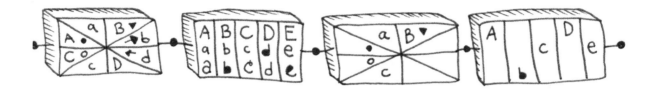
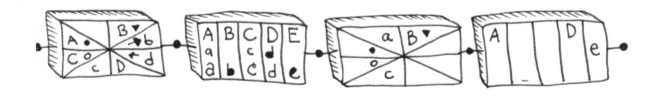
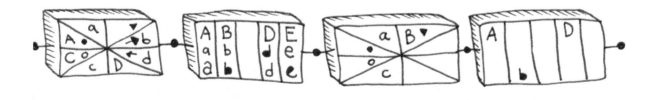
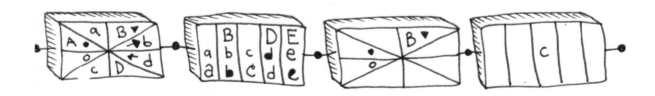

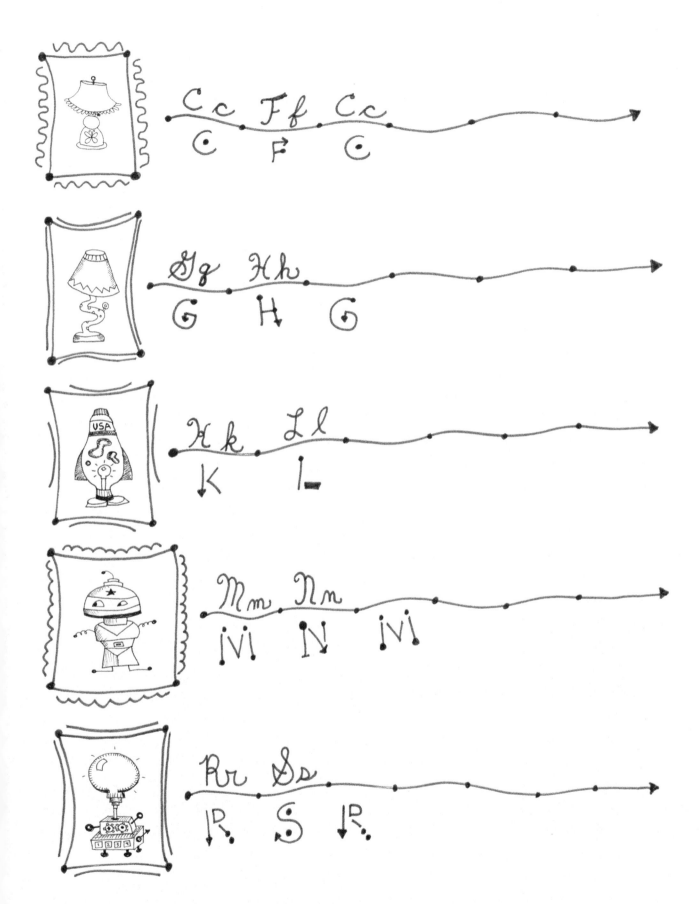

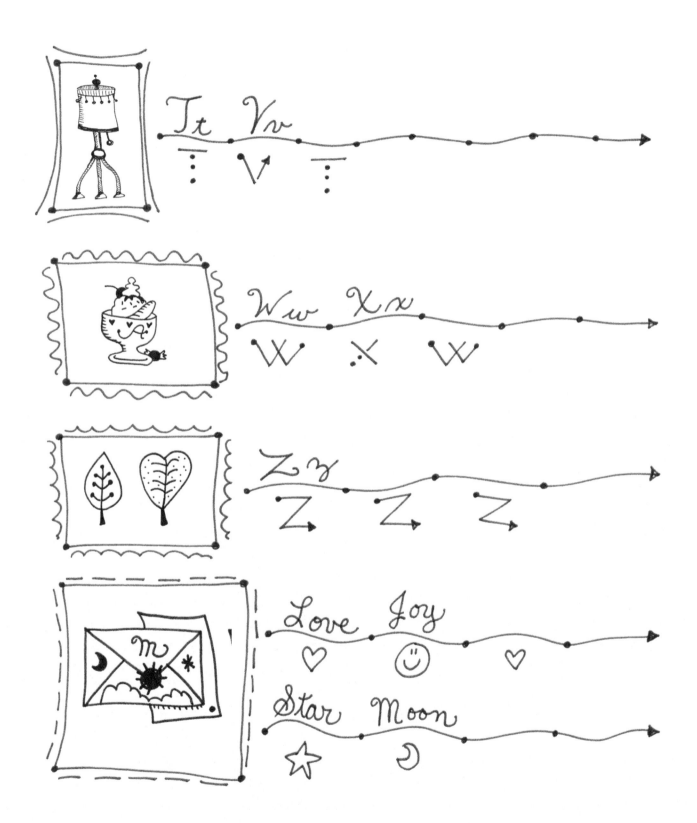

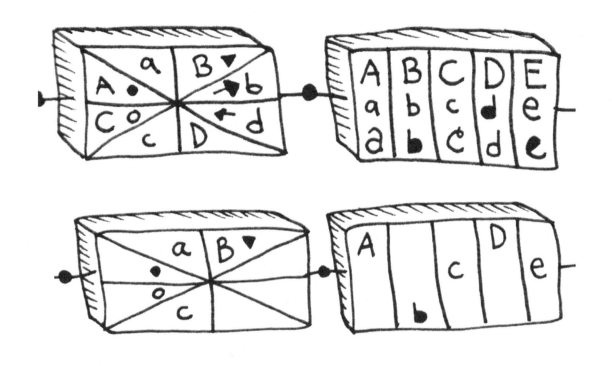

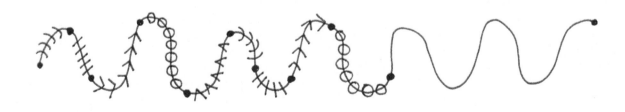

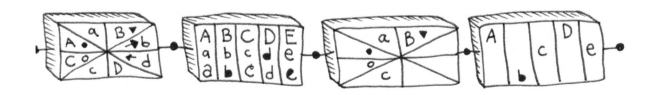

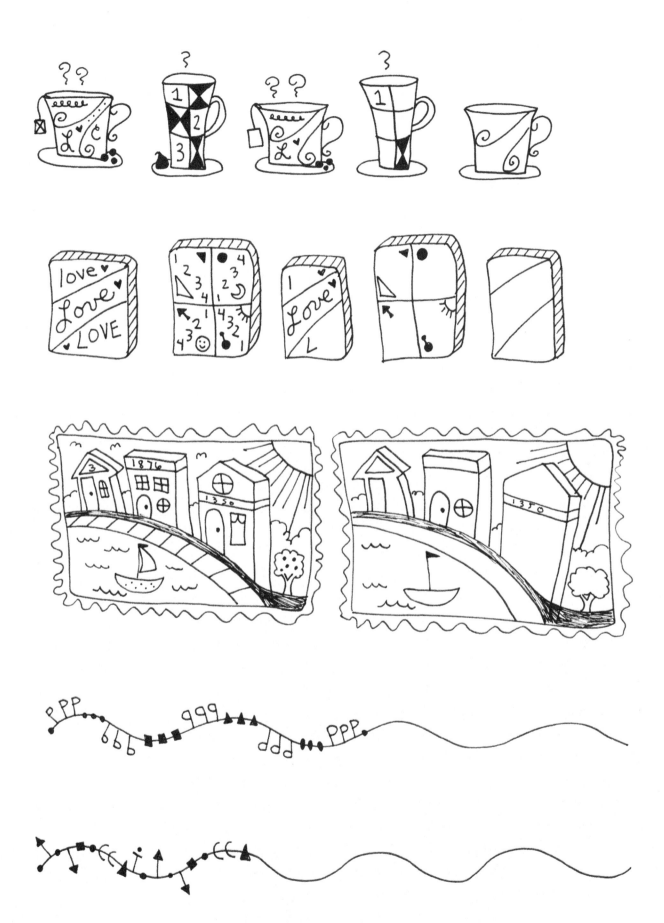

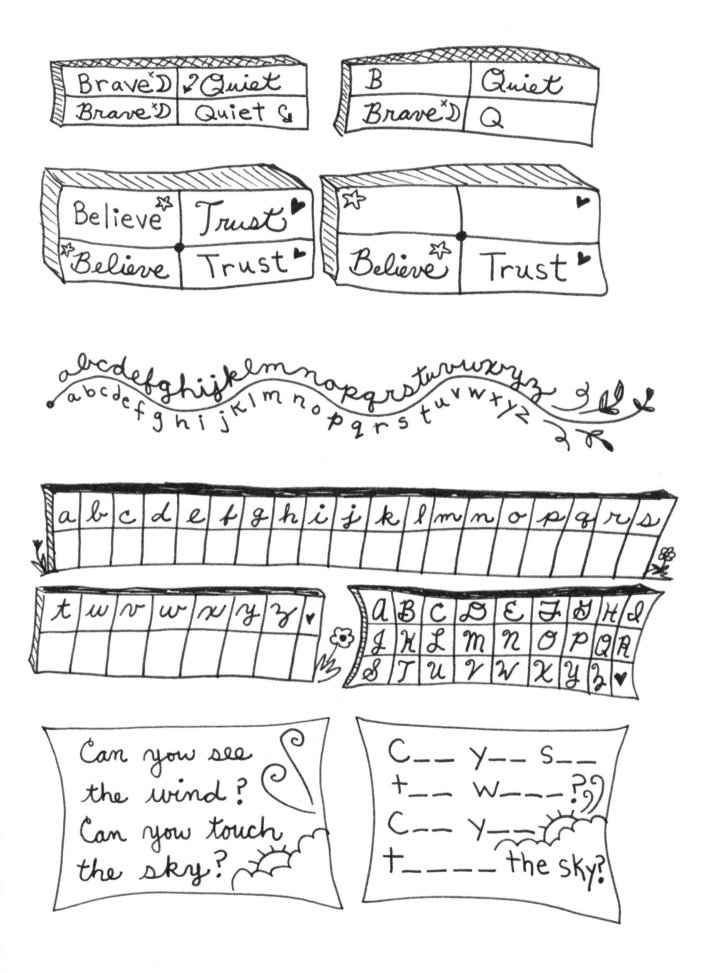

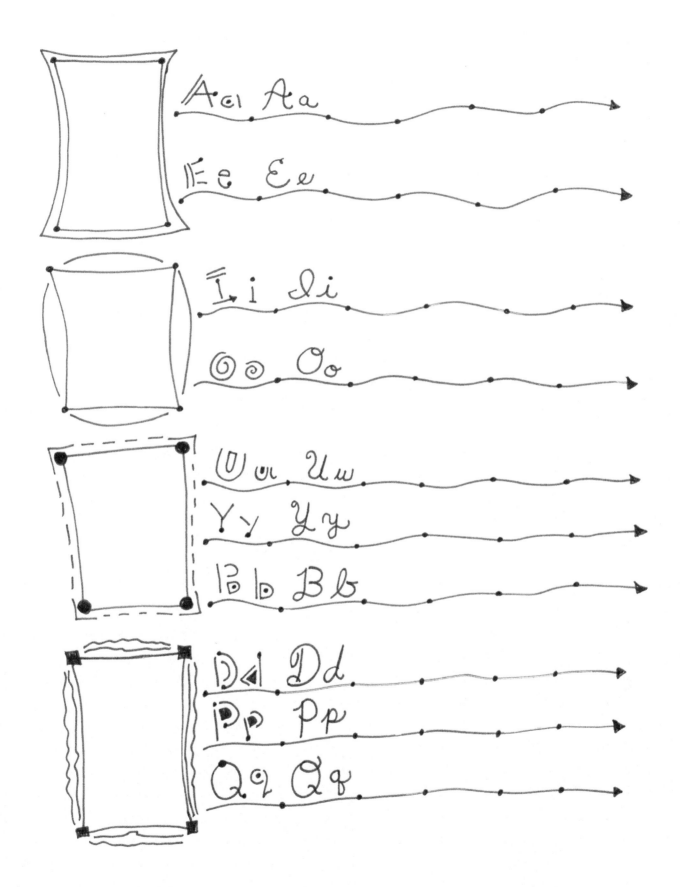

Add Colors to Each Word:

1. ABSENCE
2. ACCEPTABLE
3. ACCIDENTALLY
4. ACCOMMODATE
5. ACROSS
6. ACHIEVE
7. ACQUIRE
8. ADVERTISE
9. ADVICE

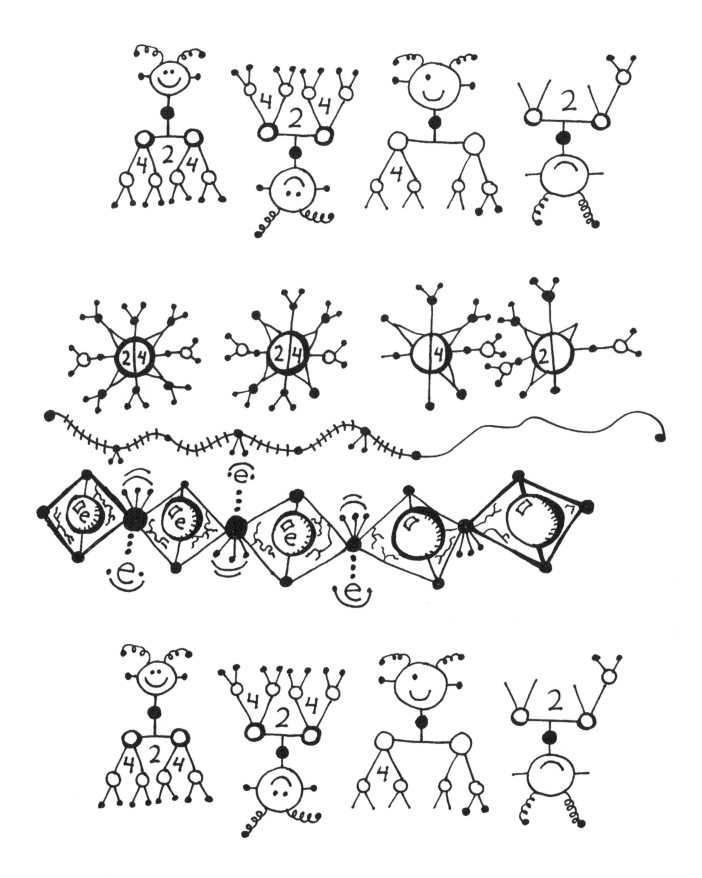

Fill in the Missing Letters:

1. ABSENCE
2. ACCEPTABLE
3. ACCIDENTALLY
4. ACCOMMODATE
5. ACROSS
6. ACHIEVE
7. ACQUIRE
8. ADVERTISE
9. ADVICE
10. ADULT
11. A LOT
12. ALMOST
13. AMATEUR
14. AMONG
15. ANNUALLY
16. APPARENT
17. ARGUMENT
18. AWFUL

1. a   en e
2. a   ept   le
3. ac   ent   ly
4. ac   mo   te
5. a   o s
6. ach   e
7. a   ui e
8. ad   rt e
9. a vi e
10. a   lt
11. a   t
12. a   st
13. am   r
14. a   ng
15. an   l y
16. ap   r nt
17. ar   m   nt
18. a   l

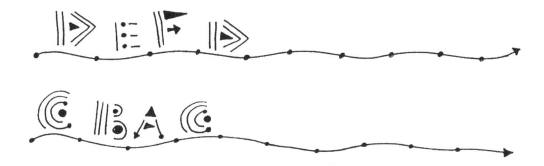

Add Colors to Each Word:

1. ADULT
2. A LOT
3. ALMOST
4. AMATEUR
5. AMONG
6. ANNUALLY
7. APPARENT
8. ARGUMENT
9. AWFUL

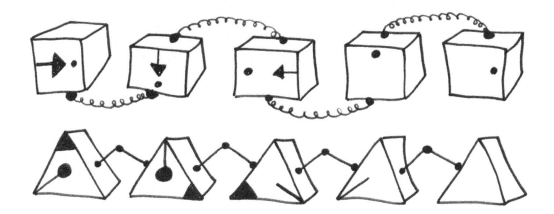

Fill in the Missing Letters:

1. absence	1. ab___ce	1. ab_____
2. acceptable	2. a___ptable	2. ac_____e
3. accidentally	3. ac___entally	3. ac_____ly
4. accommodate	4. accom___ate	4. ac_____te
5. across	5. ac___s	5. a____s
6. achieve	6. ac___ve	6. a_____e
7. acquire	7. a___ire	7. a_____e
8. advertise	8. adver___e	8. a_____e
9. advice	9. ad___e	9. a____e
10. adult	10. a__lt	10. a____
11. a lot	11. a l__	11. a ___
12. almost	12. al___t	12. a____t
13. amateur	13. ama___r	13. a_____r
14. among	14. a___g	14. a____
15. annually	15. a___ally	15. an_____
16. apparent	16. ap___ent	16. ap_____
17. argument	17. arg___nt	17. ar_____
18. awful	18. a___l	18. a____

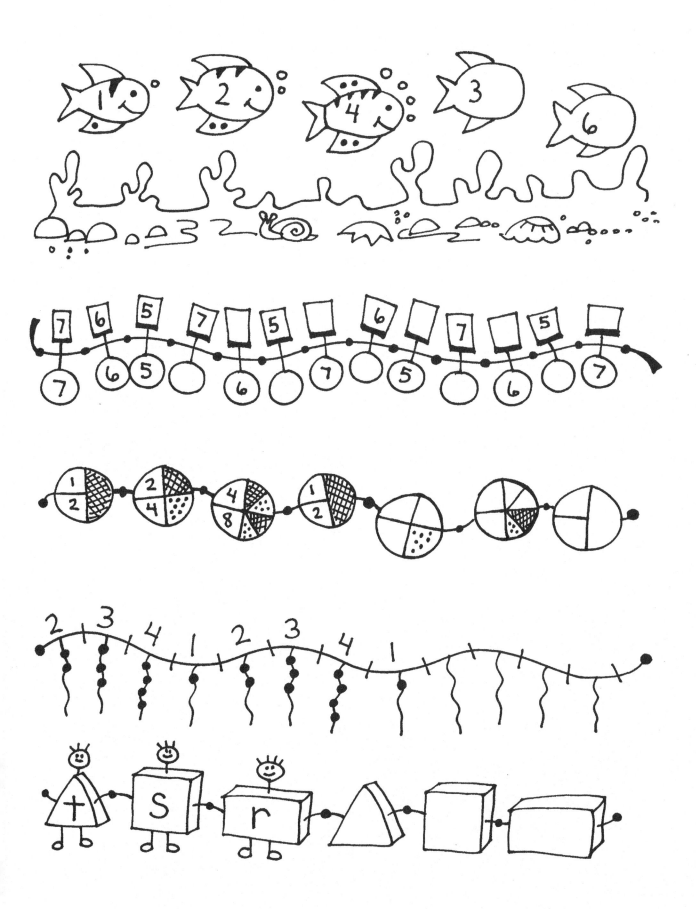

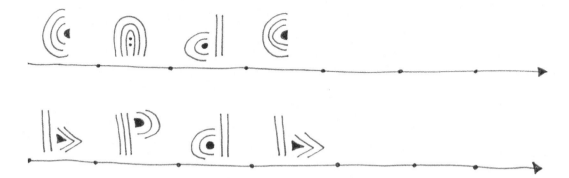

Add Colors to Each Word:

1. BALANCE
2. BECOMING
3. BEFORE
4. BELIEVE
5. BREATHE
6. BRILLIANT
7. BUSINESS
8. BURGLAR

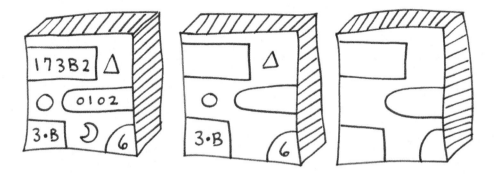

Write in the Missing Words or Letters:

1. BALANCE
2. BECOMING
3. BEFORE
4. BELIEVE
5. BREATHE
6. BRILLIANT
7. BUSINESS
8. BURGLAR
9. CALENDAR
10. CAREFUL
11. CATEGORY
12. CHANGEABLE
13. CITIZEN
14. COLLECTIBLE
15. COLUMN
16. COMING
17. COMMITTED
18. COMPETITION
19. CONSCIENCE
20. CONSCIOUS
21. CONVENIENCE
22. CRITICIZE

1. BAL NCE
2.
3. BEFO E
4.
5. BR ATHE
6.
7. BUSINE S
8. BU GLAR
9.
10. CAR FUL
11.
12. CHANGE BLE
13.
14. COLLECT LE
15. COL N
16.
17. COM IT ED
18.
19. CONSC NCE
20. CO SC US
21.
22. CRIT CI E

Add Colors to Each Word:

1. CALENDAR
2. CAREFUL
3. CATEGORY
4. CHANGEABLE
5. CITIZEN
6. COLLECTIBLE
7. COLUMN
8. COMING
9. COMMITTED
10. COMPETITION
11. CONSCIENCE
12. CONSCIOUS
13. CONVENIENCE
14. CRITICIZE

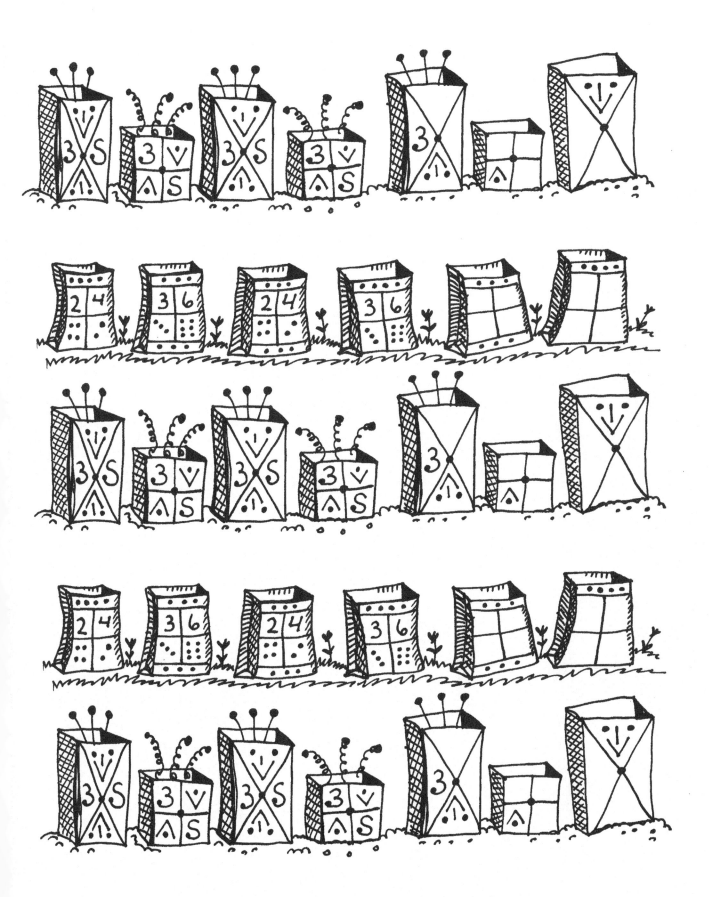

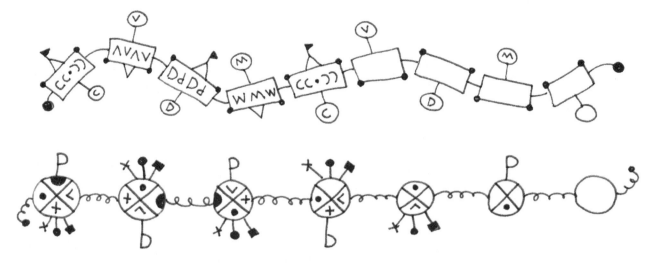

Write in the Missing Words:

1. balance	1. balance	1. _____
2. becoming	2. becoming	2. _____
3. before	3. before	3. _____
4. believe	4. believe	4. _____
5. breathe	5. breathe	5. _____
6. brilliant	6. brilliant	6. _____
7. business	7. business	7. _____
8. burglar	8. burglar	8. _____
9. calendar	9. calendar	9. _____
10. careful	10. careful	10. _____
11. category	11. category	11. _____
12. changeable	12. changeable	12. _____
13. citizen	13. citizen	13. _____
14. collectible	14. collectible	14. _____
15. column	15. column	15. _____
16. coming	16. coming	16. _____
17. committed	17. committed	17. _____
18. competition	18. competition	18. _____
19. conscience	19. conscience	19. _____
20. conscious	20. conscious	20. _____
21. convenience	21. convenience	21. _____
22. criticize	22. criticize	22. _____

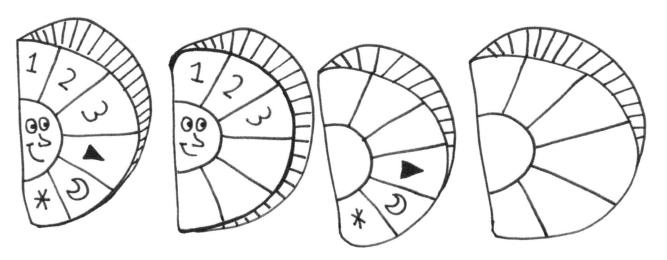

Add Colors to Each Word:

1. DESCRIBE
2. DECIDE
3. DECEIVE
4. DEFINITE
5. DEFINITELY
6. DEVELOP
7. DISCIPLINE
8. DOES
9. DURING

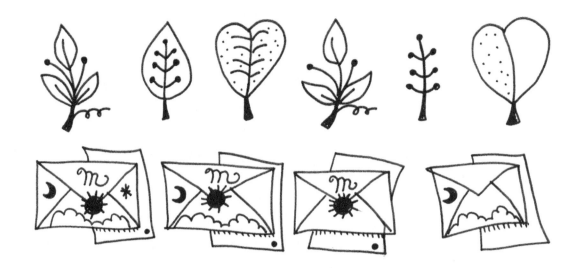

Fill in the Missing Letters:

1. DESCRIBE
2. DECIDE
3. DECEIVE
4. DEFINITE
5. DEFINITELY
6. DEVELOP
7. DISCIPLINE
8. DOES
9. DURING
10. EASILY
11. EIGHT
12. EITHER
13. EMBARRASS
14. EQUIPMENT
15. EXHILARATE
16. EXCEED
17. EXCELLENT
18. EXERCISE
19. EXISTENCE
20. EXPERIENCE

1. des ri e
2. de i e
3. de e ve
4. de in te
5. de in t ly
6. d ve op
7. di ci l ne
8. do s
9. d r ng
10. e s ly
11. e g t
12. e th r
13. emb rr ss
14. eq ipm nt
15. exh l r te
16. exc ed
17. exc ll nt
18. ex rc se
19. ex st nce
20. exp r ence

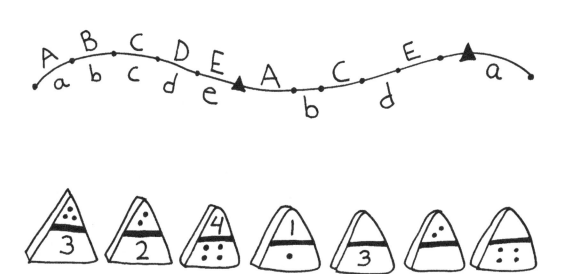
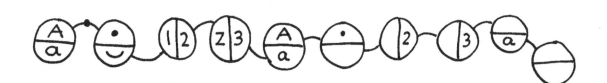
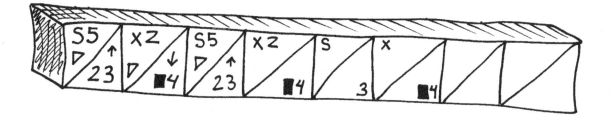

Add Colors to Each Word:

1. EASILY
2. EIGHT
3. EITHER
4. EMBARRASS
5. EQUIPMENT
6. EXHILARATE
7. EXCEED
8. EXCELLENT
9. EXERCISE
10. EXISTENCE
11. EXPERIENCE

Write in the Missing Words:

1.	1. DESCRIBE	1. describe
2. decide	2.	2. decide
3. deceive	3. DECEIVE	3.
4.	4. DEFINITE	4. definite
5. definitely	5.	5. definitely
6. develop	6. DEVELOP	6.
7.	7. DISCIPLINE	7. discipline
8. does	8.	8. does
9. during	9. DURING	9.
10.	10. EASILY	10. easily
11. eight	11.	11. eight
12. either	12. EITHER	12.
13.	13. EMBARRASS	13. embarrass
14. equipment	14.	14. equipment
15. exhilarate	15. EXHILARATE	15.
16.	16. EXCEED	16. exceed
17. excellent	17.	17. excellent
18. exercise	18. EXERCISE	18.
19.	19. EXISTENCE	19. existence
20. experience	20.	20. experience

G H I G

J K L J

Add Colors to Each Word:

1. FAMILIAR
2. FINALLY
3. FOREIGN
4. FORTY
5. FRIEND
6. GOVERNMENT
7. GRAMMAR
8. GRATEFUL
9. GUARANTEE

Add Colors to Each Word:

1. HAPPINESS
2. HARASS
3. HEIGHT
4. HEROES
5. HUMOROUS
6. IGNORANCE
7. IMMEDIATE
8. INDEPENDENT
9. INTELLIGENCE
10. INTERESTING
11. ISLAND

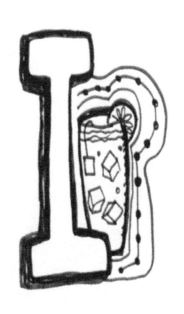

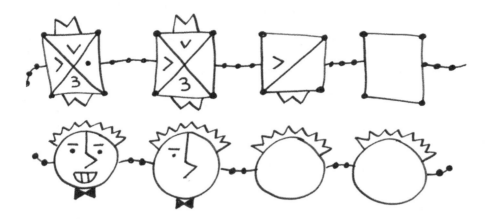

Fill in the Missing Letters:

1. familiar	1. famil ar	1. fa ar
2. finally	2. f nally	2. f ly
3. foreign	3. fore gn	3. fo n
4. forty	4. f rty	4. f y
5. friend	5. fri nd	5. f nd
6. government	6. gov rnm nt	6. gover nt
7. grammar	7. gr mm r	7. gram r
8. grateful	8. gr t ful	8. gr ful
9. guarantee	9. gu r nt e	9. gua tee
10. happiness	10. h pp n ss	10. hap ess
11. harass	11. h r ss	11. ha s
12. height	12. he ght	12. h ht
13. heroes	13. hero s	13. he s
14. humorous	14. hum ro s	14. hum us
15. ignorance	15. ign r nce	15. ignor e
16. immediate	16. imm di te	16. i diate
17. independent	17. ind p nd nt	17. inde dent
18. intelligence	18. int ll g nce	18. in nce
19. interesting	19. int r st ng	19. int ing
20. island	20. i l nd	20. i d

Add Colors to Each Word:

1. JEALOUS
2. JEWELRY
3. JUDGMENT
4. KERNEL
5. KNOWLEDGE
6. LEISURE
7. LESSON
8. LIAISON
9. LIBERTY
10. LIBRARY
11. LICENSE
12. LYING

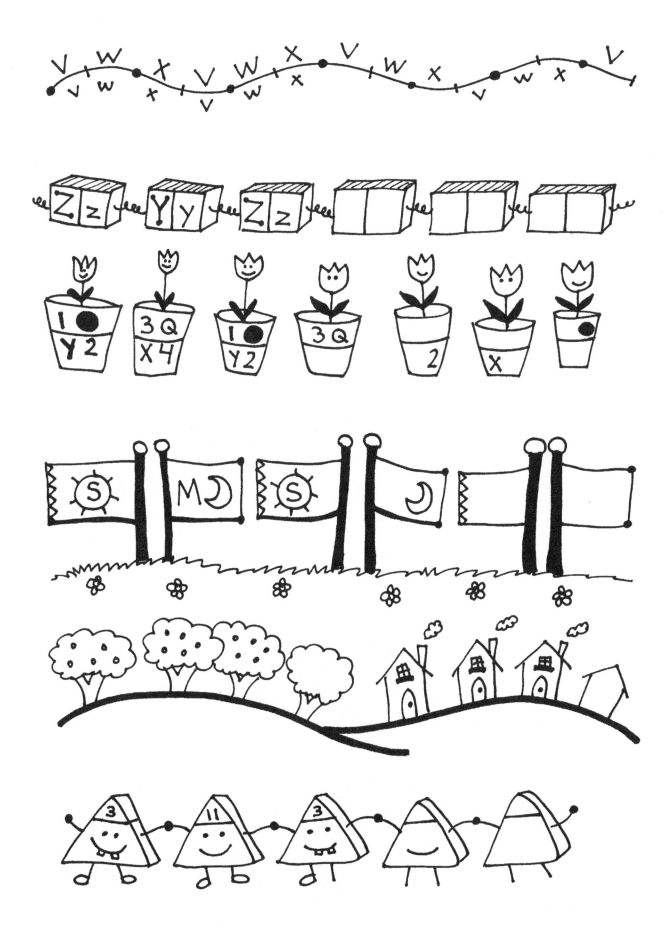

Fill in the Missing Vowels:

1. jealous
2. jewelry
3. judgment
4. kernel
5. knowledge
6. leisure
7. lesson
8. liaison
9. liberty
10. library
11. license
12. lying

1. j l s
2. j w lry
3. j dgm nt
4. k rn l
5. kn wl dg
6. l s r
7. l ss n
8. l s n
9. l b rty
10. l br ry
11. l c ns
12. ly ng

Add Colors to Each Word:

1. MAINTENANCE
2. MANEUVER
3. MARRIAGE
4. MEDIEVAL
5. MILLENNIUM
6. MINIATURE
7. MINUTE
8. MISCHIEVOUS
9. MISSPELL

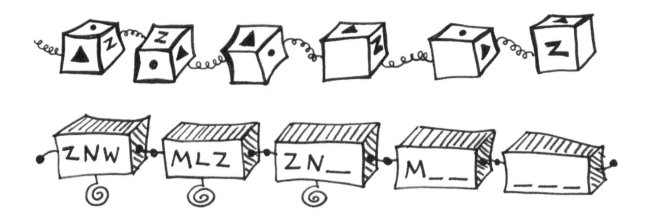

Fill in the Missing Vowels:

1. maintenance
2. maneuver
3. marriage
4. medieval
5. millennium
6. miniature
7. minute
8. mischievous
9. misspell

1. m nt n nc
2. m n v r
3. m rr g
4. m d v l
5. m ll nn m
6. m n t r
7. m n t
8. m sch v s
9. m ssp ll

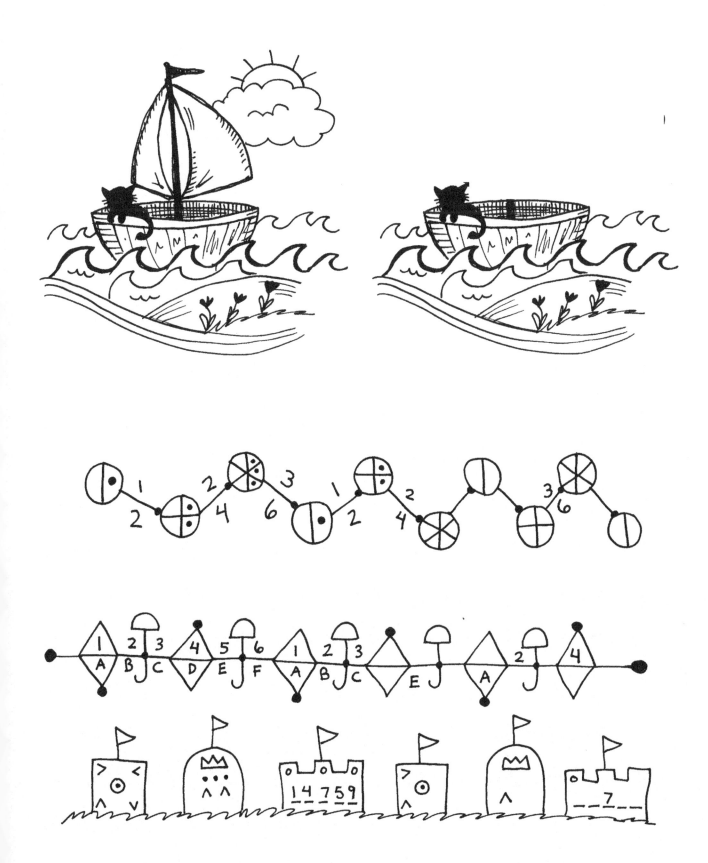

Add Colors to Each Word:

1. NEIGHBOR
2. NOTICEABLE
3. OCCASION
4. OCCASIONALLY
5. OCCURRENCE
6. OFFICIAL
7. OFTEN

Write in the Missing Words:

1. NEIGHBOR	1.	1. neighbor
2. NOTICEABLE	2. noticeable	2.
3. OCCASION	3.	3. occasion
4. OCCASIONALLY	4. occasionally	4.
5. OCCURRENCE	5.	5. occurrence
6. OFFICIAL	6. official	6. official
7. OFTEN	7.	7. often
8. PAID	8. paid	8.
9. PERFORM	9.	9. perform
10. PERSEVERANCE	10. perseverance	10.
11. PICTURE	11.	11. picture
12. POSSESSION	12. possession	12.
13. PRECEDE	13.	13. precede
14. PRINCIPAL	14.	14. principal
15. PRINCIPLE	15. principle	15.
16. PRIVILEGE	16.	16. privilege
17. PRONUNCIATION	17. pronunciation	17.
18. PUBLICLY	18.	18. publicly

Add Colors to Each Word:

1. PAID
2. PERFORM
3. PERSEVERANCE
4. PICTURE
5. POSSESSION
6. PRECEDE
7. PRINCIPAL
8. PRINCIPLE
9. PRIVILEGE
10. PRONUNCIATION
11. PUBLICLY

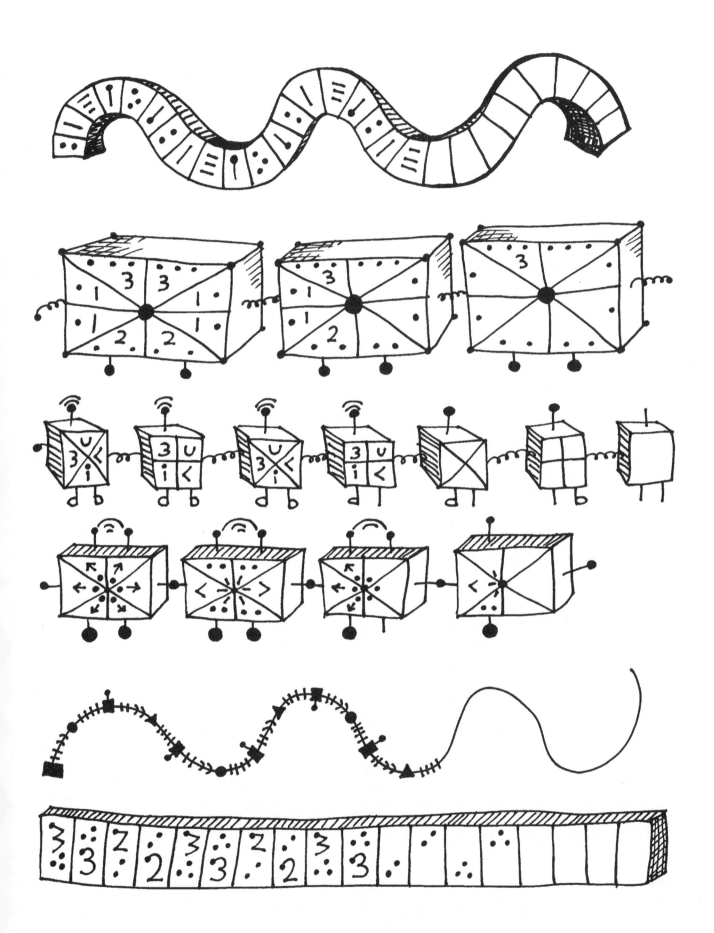

Add Colors to Each Word:

1. QUIET
2. REALIZE
3. RECEIVE
4. RECEIPT
5. RECOMMEND
6. REFERRED
7. REFERENCE
8. RELEVANT
9. RESTAURANT
10. RHYME
11. RHYTHM

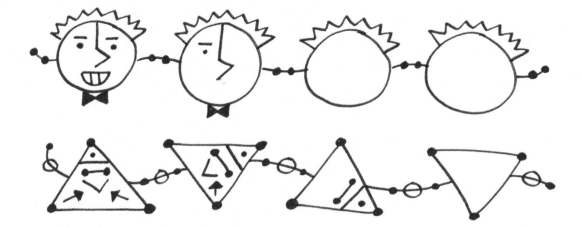

Fill in the Missing Vowels:

1. quiet
2. realize
3. receive
4. receipt
5. recommend
6. referred
7. reference
8. relevant
9. restaurant
10. rhyme
11. rhythm
12. safety
13. schedule
14. scissors
15. separate
16. speech
17. surprise

1. qu t
2. r l z
3. r c v
4. r c pt
5. r c mm nd
6. r f rr d
7. r f r nc
8. r l v nt
9. r st r nt
10. rh m
11. rh thm
12. s f ty
13. sch d l
14. sc ss rs
15. s p r t
16. sp ch
17. s rpr s

Add Colors to Each Word:

1. SAFETY
2. SCHEDULE
3. SCISSORS
4. SEPARATE
5. SPEECH
6. SURPRISE

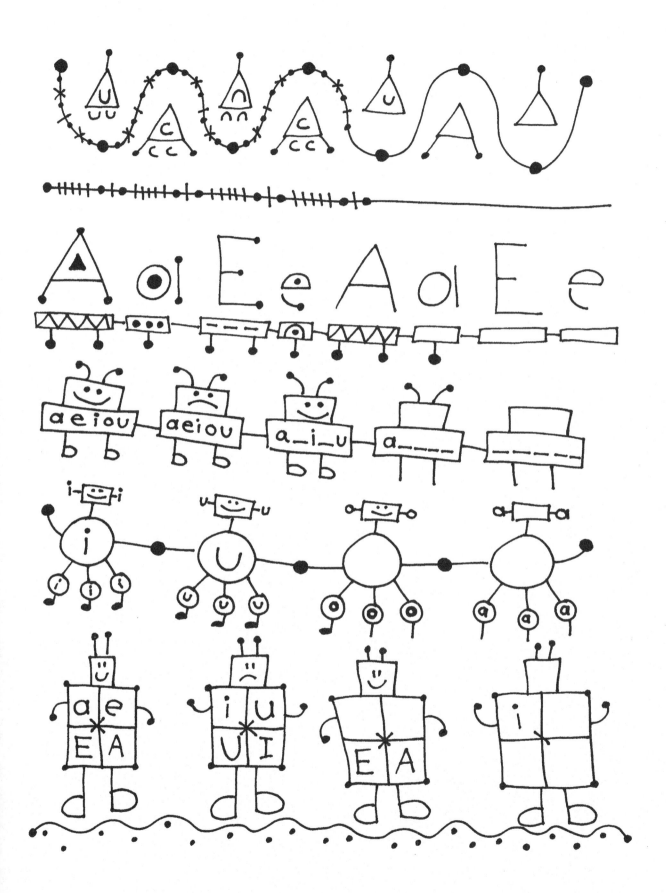

Add Colors to Each Word:

1. THEIR
2. THEY'RE
3. THERE
4. TOWARD
5. TRULY
6. TWELFTH

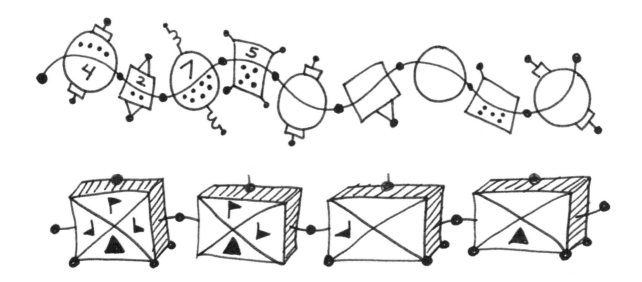

Fill in the Missing Letters:

1. TH R	1. THEIR	1. T R
2. TH 'RE	2. THEY'RE	2. T 'RE
3. TH RE	3. THERE	3. T E
4. TO RD	4. TOWARD	4. T D
5. TR Y	5. TRULY	5. T Y
6. T LFTH	6. TWELFTH	6. T H
7. UN L	7. UNTIL	7. U L
8. U SUAL	8. UNUSUAL	8. U L
9. USU LY	9. USUALLY	9. U Y
10. VA UM	10. VACUUM	10. V M
11. V LAGE	11. VILLAGE	11. V E
12. WE HER	12. WEATHER	12. W R
13. W RD	13. WEIRD	13. W D

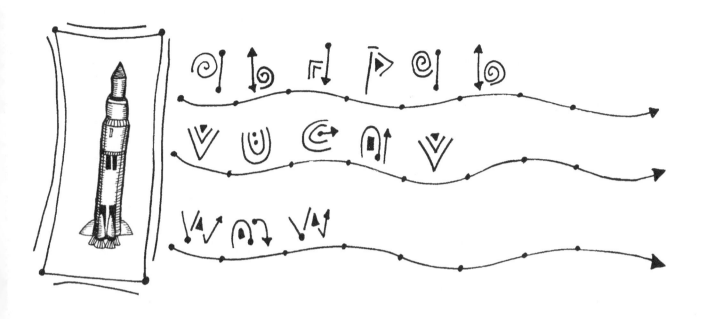

Add Colors to Each Word:

1. UNTIL
2. UNUSUAL
3. USUALLY
4. VACUUM
5. VILLAGE
6. WEATHER
7. WEIRD

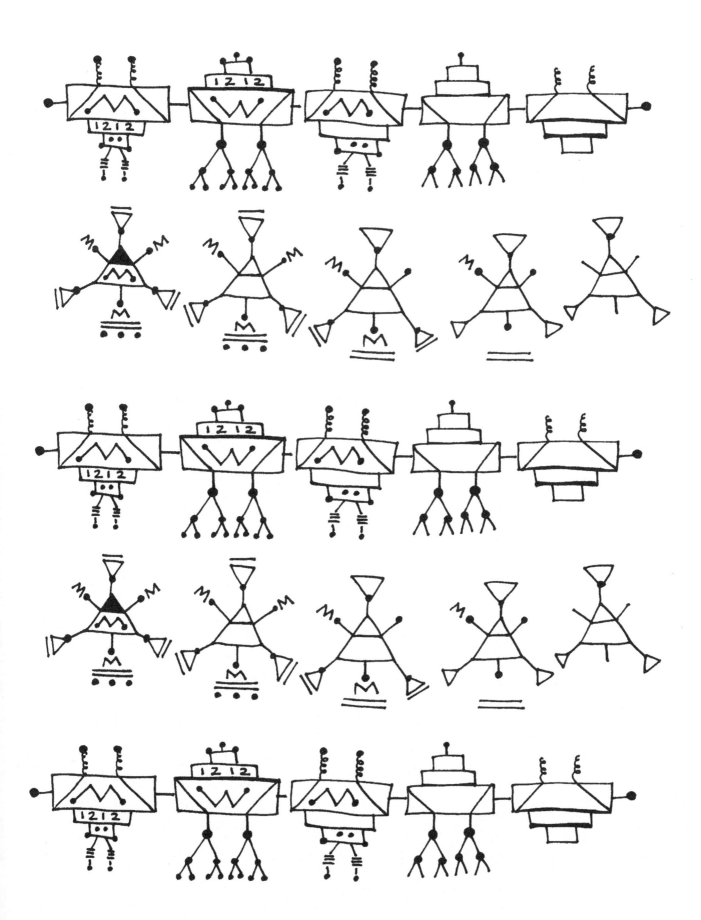

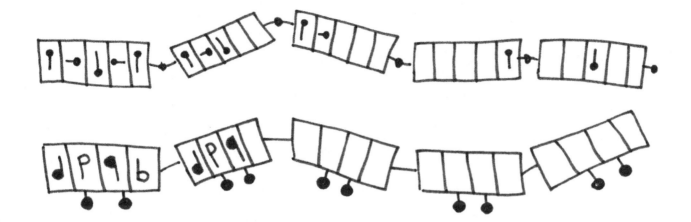

Write in the Missing Words:

1. their
2. _____
3. there
4. _____
5. truly
6. _____
7. until
8. _____
9. usually
10. _____
11. village
12. _____
13. weird

1. _____
2. they're
3. _____
4. toward
5. _____
6. twelfth
7. _____
8. unusual
9. _____
10. vacuum
11. _____
12. weather
13. _____

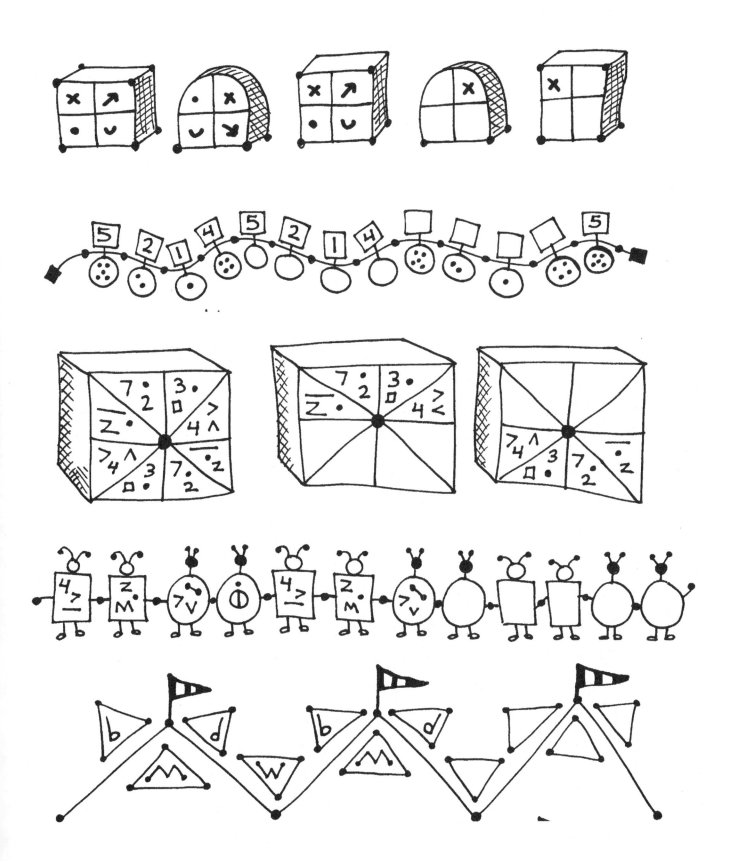

Sarah Janisse Brown
Blog: FunschoolingWithSarah.com
Bookstore: Funschooling.com

Made in United States
Orlando, FL
11 May 2024

46538116R00076